PHINEAS TAYLOR BARNUM:

The Greatest Humbug on Earth

THE HISTORY HOUR

CONTENTS

❧ I ❧

INTRODUCTION

❧

In any culture, it is often argued, there are a small number of people who shape it by virtue of their strength of character, their fortitude, and perhaps because of their weaknesses. American culture as we know it today was started when Puritans landed on Plymouth Rock, persecuted, executed, and annihilated the Native Peoples. The Protestant and evangelical ethic was a strong part of the founding bedrock of American society, but in the eighteenth century, there were a group of philosophers, politicians, inventors, and writers - the likes of Alexander Hamilton, Benjamin Franklin, George Washington, and John Adams - who shaped the nation that later became the United States of America. These men wrote the Declaration of Independence, the Constitution and the documents that Americans seem to regard as second only to the Bible in terms of sacredness.

But the thing that gave the destiny to the America of today, the certain ineffable quality that makes America unique and magical was given to it by the big thinkers of the nineteenth century: Eli Whitney, Ralph Waldo Emerson, Emily Dickinson, Abraham Lincoln, Mark Twain, Nathaniel Hawthorne, and Henry Wadsworth Longfellow. But no single person had an influence like Phineas T. Barnum of Bridgeport, Connecticut. He was a successful small business owner, entrepreneur, newspaper editor, museum owner, sideshow operator, touring promoter for opera singers, theatrical producer, circus owner, congressman, mayor, and philanthropist. His influence on virtually every aspect of American life cannot be underestimated. It is fair to say that America as we know it today, with its waving flags, its patriotism, its odd relationship to drink and sin, its carnivalesque gaudiness, its pride could not have come to pass had it not been for the powerful voice and influence of the indefatigable P. T. Barnum. His name has been associated with circus sideshows and freaks and jokes for more than a century, but the truth is that Barnum was a great man and a visionary who shaped the country he loved so much.

❧ II ❧

WELL-SPENT YOUTH

❦

Phineas Taylor Barnum was born on July 5, 1810 – April 7, 1891 in Bethel Connecticut, to Philo Barnum and Irena Taylor. His father Philo was a farmer, a tailor, and an innkeeper with a love of jokes, and his mother's father, his namesake, known as Phineas Taylor, was an inveterate practical joker, and was P. T. Barnum's greatest influence. According to Barnum's memoir of 1855, *The Life of P. T. Barnum*, his grandfather loved nothing so much as a practical joke. And Phineas admitted to being "a chip off the old block" in that regard. His grandfather Phineas Taylor was a legislator, a landowner, a sometime justice of the peace, and (most importantly) a lottery schemer. At a very young age, he taught young Phineas the tricks of getting money without doing hard work. This became one of Barnum's great quests, as he was a very smart lad with a particular interest in arithmetic and a dislike of physical work. As

Barnum's hard working father died when Phineas was only sixteen years old, in 1826, leaving him to be the main familial breadwinner, business ventures became his stock in trade from a very early age, and most particularly those business ventures in which the purchaser felt satisfied with being ripped off.

⚜

One if Barnum's earliest business ventures was as a shop clerk when he was only fifteen years old. He was very adept at creative means of making money, learned from his grandfather, and taken to heart by the young entrepreneur. He bought a gallon of molasses and made a toffee from it, making a tidy profit. He expanded this into the orange business and other delicacies. In fact, when he was sixteen, he moved from sleepy rural Connecticut to Brooklyn New York to become a stock clerk in a store. He returned to rural Connecticut when he was seventeen, buying and running a very successful grocery store in the coach house belonging to his grandfather.

⚜

His biggest gamble Barnum took as a young man was in the field of lotteries. Barnum actually began the lottery business when he was twelve years old and kept it going as his main means of making a living until he was fifteen. At first, he had no trouble from the church going citizens of Danbury, but shortly here is where he came up against the powerful Methodist lobby to end gambling and many other pastimes that people found enjoyable. Barnum himself noted that many men of the cloth preached against the lotteries that he was running, making, as he said, two thousand dollars profit per day, but then bought tickets covertly from his store. In

the same way, he met a young seamstress named Charity
Hallett and decided he wanted to marry her. He was married
at age 19.

۞

By this time though, he was being hounded by the religious
authorities, and he found himself writing editorials
supporting the lotteries but finally decided that it was easier
to get column space by buying a newspaper of his own when
he was only twenty-one.

۞

At this time, religion was becoming very influential in politics, and while he and his family were firmly in the Democratic Party, the religious zealots, similar in disposition to
many of the zealous religious groups in almost every country,
began to harass Barnum about his lotteries. And in response,
Barnum wrote a number of articles in local newspapers, but
seeing the potential profit in taking a stand and making a
spectacle of himself, Barnum bought a printing press and
opened, at age twenty-one, *The Herald of Freedom*.

۞

Barnum himself notes that he was rash as a youth and three
times in his three years as a newspaper proprietor he was
prosecuted. Several times he accused people of being spies
and other such accusations, which made the papers, and sold
many of these papers. Sadly though, he also several times was
fined, and even once was sentenced to a period of sixty days
in a common jail. Barnum being Barnum though, he had the

cell carpeted and wallpapered and found himself there, still editing his papers.

❧

This sentence was brought down because he accused a certain "lay dignitary" from Bethel of "taking usury of an orphan boy" and this statement, although proven to be correct, (according to Barnum), was considered a serious offense, because of the use of the word usury. When he went to the jail and continued editing his paper from his cell. As a result of this stunt, he attracted a great deal of publicity, greatly increasing his newspaper subscription numbers. As a result, Barnum learned the great truth that there is no such thing as bad publicity, if spun correctly. And he spun it correctly; when he was released, he hired a brass band to accompany him home in a slow-moving procession from the jail to his home.

❧

In many ways, this unfortunate event became the very thing that began his career of publicizing odd things. The next few years would show just how good Taylor Barnum (as he was then known) could be.

✢ III ✢
THE VARIETY SHOWS

❦

In 1834, Taylor Barnum moved to New York City with his wife and four daughters because lotteries, the main source of his income, were made illegal in Connecticut. Shortly thereafter, he received a note from R. W. Lindsay in Kentucky. He claimed to have a freed slave in his household named Joice Heth, who was one hundred and sixty one years old and had been wet nurse to George Washington, the nation's first President. Barnum paid one thousand dollars to lease Joice Heth and brought her to New York (which had made slavery illegal years before) and embarked on a highly publicized tour of the Eastern seaboard of the United States from 1834-36, presenting Joice Heth for up to ten hours a day. Barnum sent out a circular to the major papers that read:

"Joice Heth is unquestionably the most astonishing

*and interesting curiosity in the World! She was
the slave of Augustine Washington, (the father
Gen. Washington) and was the first person who
put clothes on the unconscious infant, who, in
after days, led our heroic fathers on to glory, to
victory, and freedom. To use her own language
when speaking of the illustrious Father of this
Country, 'she raised him'. Joice Heth was born in
the year 1674, and has, consequently, now arrived
at the astonishing age of 161 years."*

Although Heth was blind and nearly paralyzed by this point, she told stories about "little George" and sang a hymn to the great joy of the audiences, earning Barnum as much as $1500 per week. She died in 1836 and 1500 people paid fifty cents to see the autopsy performed by Dr. David L. Rogers in the New York City Saloon. When Rogers declared that the subject was only about seventy-nine years old, Barnum declared that the real Joice Heth was on tour in Europe. He eventually admitted to the hoax.

☉⁊☋

After the death of Joice Heth, Barnum was established as a man who could draw a crowd. He established a hodge podge act known as "Barnum's Grand Scientific and Musical Theater" in which he toured theaters and music halls throughout the eastern seaboard of the United States. This was a relatively successful tour, and it allowed Barnum to hone his skills at publicity. However, in 1837, there was a severe economic depression known as the "Panic of 1837" which threw the United States into a deep financial crisis. By June 4th, 1838, Barnum disbanded his company in New Orleans and sailed for New York.

When Barnum returned to New York, he advertised that he was looking to invest in a business and that he had $2500 to contribute. He found himself inundated with ninety different offers, one less likely than the next. But then he discovered a young black dancer named John Diamond, who practiced a style of dance known as a "break-down" dance, similar to tap dancing. He connected with the father of the youth and found him an agent and watched his career take off. This unexpected success inspired him to open a tavern called the Vauxhall Garden Saloon, which provided refreshments along with singing, dancing, Yankee stories, and other entertainment. One of the most celebrated performers in this establishment was Miss Mary Taylor, who went on to become a celebrated actress and singer. By August of 1840 though, he relinquished the lease to this business and moved on, taking his group of performers on the road one more time. Once again he disbanded the company in New Orleans. Then, when he returned to his growing family, he found himself renting the Vauxhall Garden Saloon, writing advertising copy for others, and writing a host of editorials for various small newspapers.

❧ IV ❧

THE AMERICAN MUSEUM

❧❧❧

True to his temperament, Barnum viewed his new found penury as an inspiration to do better. He soon set his eyes set on bigger things.

> *"I had long fancied that I could succeed if I could only*
> *get hold of a public exhibition," Barnum wrote in*
> *1855, in his autobiography, The Life of P.T.*
> *Barnum, Written by Himself.*

He had learned, from being an outside clerk for the Bowery amphitheatre, that what he referred to as "the collection of curiosities comprising Scudder's American Museum, at the corner of Broadway and Ann Street," was being sold by its current owners, the daughters of Mr. Scudder. Although the collection of oddities was worth quite a bit, Barnum convinced the administrator, Mr. John Heath that it was only forth $12,000 because, he claimed, the building had been losing money for years.

❧

But the road to success was never as simple as that. On the appointed day when he was to sign the papers to take possession, the administrator, John Heath, informed him that it had been purchased for $15,000 and there was nothing Barnum could do about it. Barnum went to the local newspapers, informing the public that the shares in this new company were worthless. He continued to write these "squibs" in the papers until the consortium who had bought this museum agreed to sell it to him (although they first tried to buy his silence by hiring him to manage the museum).

❧

In 1841, Barnum acquired the large building on Broadway called Scudder's American Museum, which he began to suit the needs of his many human performers and the wonders he displayed. This was a five-storey marble building located at the corner of Broadway and Ann Streets in New York City. In 1841 he renovated the building and on January 1, 1842 he opened it as Barnum's American Museum.

Although this building had housed a waxworks and storage for many taxidermied animals, when Barnum bought it, he began to slowly transform it into a carnival of what were known as "freak shows", dramatic theatrical presentations, beauty contests, and other entertainments similar in flavor to the vaudeville entertainment that

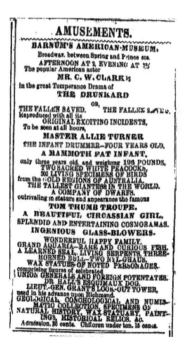

was so popular in the music halls.   Inside, there were giants, little people, fat ladies, bearded ladies, wild men from

Borneo (although, see below, they were not from Borneo, and they were not wild); freaks of various kinds both animal and human. There were people who could perform incredible feats, including juggling, magic tricks, "exotic women", and all kinds of live animals that were added to the stuffed ones. In addition, he included modern innovations, appliances, dioramas, cosmoramas, and other amazing attractions.

⚜

This museum quickly became a very popular attraction and began to shape many of the assumptions about American theater and entertainment. He installed a lighthouse light and ballyhooed it when the museum was open. This became the calling card of the American musical opening night. He also commissioned huge paintings of the marvels within its walls to be hung from the building as well as flags to be hung from the roof. The roof of the museum became an attraction in itself as a "strolling garden" with a magnificent view of the New York City skyline. From a contemporary perspective, the fact that he did not permit African Americans from attending is horrifying but from the perspective of the 1840s, segregation was actually accepted and did not raise any eyebrows. His entertainment was aimed at white people with some disposable cash, who were looking for diversion. He had no higher aspiration, not political agenda, at least not at first. This would change when the Civil War broke out.

⚜

In his memoirs, Barnum justified his work this way:

> *This is a trading world and men, women, and children who cannot live on gravity alone, need*

something to satisfy their gayer, lighter moods and hours, and he who ministers to this want is in a business established by the Author of our nature.

❦

In this way, Barnum justified his work as God's work. And there is ample evidence that he believed this strongly. He viewed his work as providing the sorts of things that heaven might offer. He gave very little thought to the cruelty of confining animals to very small cages, displaying people for their oddity, or hoodwinking audiences to enrich himself. This, in Barnum's universe, was God's work.

✹ V ✺

THE ATTRACTIONS

❦

In his museum, Barnum sought out animals, things and people that would intrigue the general public. He used advertising campaigns mainly through local newspapers that involved publicity stunts, lawsuits, and repetitive advertising to elicit international acclaim for his museum.

❦

Among the one hundred and eighty thousand attractions, shows, and curiosities there was a flea circus, a loom run by a dog, an oyster bar, a rifle range, and humbugs like the so-called "Feejee Mermaid", a monkey's torso with a fish's tail grafted onto it. There was a seal named Ned who was supposedly able to reason, a beluga whale who was housed in a small tank in the basement of the museum, ventriloquists, trained bears presented by that most famous of humbuggers, "Grizzly" Adams, and a number of strange human attractions. Some of these included Chang and Eng Bunker (1811-74), the original Siamese twins, many groups of Indigenous Americans who performed traditional songs and dances, magicians of all sorts, and black-face minstrel shows. Like all minstrel shows at that time, they were presented by white people who had applied black-face make-up to their faces, and presented broad stereotypes of African American people. Later on, he would employ black actors who nevertheless also applied blackface make-up to make them seem more black. There is a strange aesthetic in the minstrel show. Generally speaking these shows were humorous takes on the state of black-white relations. The "interlocutor" character, ostensibly the more intelligent of the characters, would present an argument similar to those claimed by whites to assert their superiority. At least in theory, this would present the all-white audience with a version of a critique of this axiomatic belief. In one such show, an interlocutor would give a parody lecture in the form of a stump speech of a phrenologist (a humbug of the nineteenth century medical quackery which involved a study of the bumps on a person's head) trying to prove the superiority of the white race.

> *"You see den, dat clebber man and dam rascal means*
> *de same in Dutch, when dey boph white; but*
> *when one white and de udder's black, dat's a grey*
> *hoss ob anoder color."*

Humorous or not, (and to today's audiences, this is seldom viewed as funny), there is a certain irony presented, a certain means by which an alternate perspective is admitted into the discourse. Barnum claimed that he was only interested in the humor of this situation, but his activities were strongly supportive of Unionist political views, including the support of the emancipation proclamation.

❀

Some of the people who made up his freak show included Charles Stratton (1838-83), also known as "General Tom Thumb." In 1842, Charles Stratton, a four year old boy was brought by his parents to Barnum, claiming that he stopped growing when he was six months old. He was only 25 inches high and weighed 15 lbs, when he was brought by his parents to see Barnum. Barnum taught him sing, dance and imitate famous people like Napoleon and other great figures from history, and gave him the stage name of General Tom Thumb after the old English fairytale. He told everyone that Stratton was 11 years old. Tom Thumb was incredibly adept at learning and Barnum himself trained him to speak in many languages and accents, to recite poems and scenes, and to create scenarios that caused a sensation in the museum. Stratton, as General Tom Thumb quickly became a superstar and was a wealthy man when he was still a minor, owning his own mansion and yacht. For his part, by the 1850s, Barnum had become one of the wealthiest men in New York largely because of the popularity of General Tom Thumb.

※

The sisters Minnie (1849-78) and her younger sister Lavinia Warren (1842-1919) had a pituitary disorder that made them very small, but proportionate dwarfs. Although born seven years apart, they were nevertheless marketed as twin sisters. Lavinia was an accomplished actress who went on to perform in a silent film called *The Lilliputian's Courtship* (1915). She married General Tom Thumb, while her elder sister Minnie married George Washington Morrison "Commodore" Nutt, another proportionate dwarf performer, in 1865, but sadly died from complications during childbirth in 1878. President

Abraham Lincoln was a big fan of the little people, and invited them to the White House.

⚜

Myrtle Corben, known as the four-legged girl, earned about four hundred and fifty dollars per week in the 1850s, which is about $11,000 per week in modern money. She began touring with Barnum when she was thirteen years old and was married when she was 19, having five children.

"Zip, the Pinhead": William Henry Johnson was from a family of former slaves, and suffered from microcephaly, which made him mentally challenged. Barnum put him in a cage and marketed him as the missing link between apes and humans. Johnson spoke only in a language Barnum himself invented.

"Prince Randian," from Guyana, was called the human torso. He had no arms or legs, and was able to do a number of tricks and he was popular because of his great sense of humor. He was married and had five children and went on to appear in the 1932 film *Freaks*.

⚜

"The Wild Men of Borneo" were Hiram and Barney Davis,

two diminutive and mentally challenged men. Although they only weighed about forty pounds and were less than five feet tall, they were marketed as "Waino and Plutanor, The Wild Men of Borneo", even though they were not from Borneo. These men lived well into their nineties and were able to live well for the rest of their lives, because of

WAINO AND PLUTANOR.
Aged about 30 years.   Weight 45 pounds each.
Syracuse Univ. Library, Special Collections

huge amount of money they earned in Barnum's New American Museum.

※

Josephine Clofullia, known as the bearded lady, was born in Switzerland in 1827. In 1853, Barnum hired a man named William Charle to sue him for fraud to prove that Josephine was in fact a woman and not just a man in a dress. Her father, her husband and three doctors confirmed that she was a woman.

Chang Yu Sing, the "Chinese Giant," was over eight feet tall, (and marketed as nine feet tall). Barnum dressed him in flowing robes to give the illusion of height. He only performed for a short time with Barnum, but was a very popular act, appearing with very small people to accentuate his height.

Isaac W. Sprague was known as the "human skeleton" who was a very thin former cobbler who was so thin because of a condition he had, that he resembled a skeleton.

What stands out in the study of Barnum's peculiar idea for entertainment, as distinct from the way other promoters of even normal acts like singers and vaudeville entertainers, is the fact that he paid his performers very well. These people, many of whom would not be able to earn a normal living under normal circumstances because of their difference, were lauded and appreciated *because* of their difference. They were paid sufficiently well that they could retire in dignity rather than be tossed out as a "freak" which was the fate of many of these people before Barnum. One could argue that this is a barbaric practice, using and displaying these poor people for their oddity, but never in the history of humankind have so many differently abled people been appreciated and rewarded for their difference.

❧

In addition to these people, there were theatrical shows, lectures, demonstrations, and all kinds of other attractions. Admission to the museum was only twenty-five cents, and so the museum quickly filled up so that he could not admit a single other person. Barnum's solution was to put up, without fanfare, signs that said "This way to the egress" which led to a door that, when

THIS WAY TO
THE EGRESS

opened, would lock behind the patron, leaving them in an alley. Once they discovered the ruse, they would need to pay again to get back into the museum. Barnum reported that nearly half the people who went out the egress (which is another word for exit) would pay to see the egress again, thinking they had made a mistake.

⚜

Every one of the attractions in Barnum's Museum was what he described as a humbug. A humbug, in nineteenth century terms, was "a glittering performance, and outside show, with novel expedients by which to suddenly arrest public attention and attract the public eye and ear." It is interesting to note that the truth or falsehood of each attraction was of very little interest to Barnum. He was more concerned with the appearance of value for money from the perspective of the viewer. Although he claimed that the two famous quips associated with him were not said by him, they do effectively sum up his attitude to entertainment:

> *"there's a sucker born every minute" (which he never*
> *actually said or wrote) and, more interestingly,*
> *"nobody ever went broke underestimating the*
> *American public."*

⚜

Barnum's interest in titillating his public was rewarded a thousand fold, and in 1849, he opened a second museum in Philadelphia, which he gave over to a very efficient manager who ran it successfully until 1851 when he sold it for a small fortune.

❧ VI ❧
JENNY LIND

Although Barnum was, by any standard, a highly successful entrepreneur, he still sought legitimacy from those whom he regarded as his social superiors. Social capital was a highly prized item to the New World's greatest showman, partly because of his relatively humble beginnings, and partly because of his interest in bettering both himself and his customers. He had a perception, real or imagined that he was thought of as a rather disreputable nouveau riche boor, and he was very attracted to the high art credentials of people like Miss Jenny Lind, and her famed kindness and charity. Of course, at this time, Barnum had never even heard of Jenny Lind, despite her fame in Europe. In order to gain this valued social capital that a person like Lind could provide, Barnum began to frequent the opera in New York. He became aware of the wealth of entertainment available here and began to look for something that would legitimize him in the eyes of America's gentry. While he was a very wealthy man, and his wealth was steadily increasing, he wanted to be associated with something European, something tasteful.

※※

By a remarkable stroke of good timing, the great Swedish soprano opera singer Jenny Lind, the "Swedish Nightingale" who had been the most popular singer in Europe for fourteen years, close with such composers as Felix Mendelssohn and Giacomo Meyerbeer, announced her retirement from the operatic stage at age twenty-nine, in 1850. Jenny Lind had been a popular singer for over a decade, and was well acquainted with the greatest composers of the day including Felix Mendelssohn and Giacomo Meyerbeer, both of whom wrote music for her. She was in the middle of her third triumphant season in London England, when Barnum began to take note of her ability to attract large crowds. Although Barnum admitted to being unmusical and had never heard of Jenny Lind and never heard her sing before, he nevertheless wanted to bring her to America, because of the perceived value she had as an attraction.

Some of the attractive elements of Jenny Lind to Barnum were her interest in charity and her perceived kindness to those weaker than her. The fact is, Jenny Lind, like Barnum, had come from relatively humble beginnings. She benefited from the tutelage of the free schools in Stockholm Sweden, and consequently, she wanted to return some money to these schools. Lind already had a great reputation as a philanthropist and so when Barnum engaged Englishman John Wilton to contact her and offer her the as-yet unheard of sum of $1,000 plus expenses per concert for up to one hundred and fifty concerts in a year, she accepted, knowing this money would be a huge help to the schools. From Barnum's perspective, it was yet another selling point for the great singer.

When Jenny Lind heard this offer, she found it difficult to believe at first. To convince her that this was not some fly by night offer from a showman, she went to a London bank to try to verify that Barnum was not a crank, and that he in fact had the money he was offering her. Although she was tempted to accept the offer, she also insisted that she have the finest musicians in the world, including the acclaimed German conductor and pianist Julius Benedict as her accompanist, and Italian baritone Giovanni Belletti as her assisting artist, with whom she would sing duets. Benedict asked for and received twenty-five thousand dollars for the tour from Barnum, also paid up-front, and Belletti received twelve thousand, five hundred dollars.

Lind's contract stipulated that the entire fee for the year was to be deposited in advance to the Baring Brothers' bank in London, England. This was a very large hardship for Barnum, who, although he was known for paying his artists well, was similarly used to paying them after their performances were complete. Thus he sought loans from various bankers in New York, none of whom would lend him the money based on a percentage of the Lind tour. In order to make the tour happen, he was forced to mortgage all of his commercial and residential properties. Despite all this, Barnum was not able to raise the necessary $187,500 US and sought a loan of the final $5000 from a Philadelphia minister who thought that the appearance of Jenny Lind in America would be good for the morals of Americans. Lind then signed the contract to give one hundred and fifty concerts in a year (or eighteen months), with the option to withdraw from the agreement after either sixty or one hundred concerts, paying Barnum back $25,000 for the inconvenience.

❁

Barnum hired a large number of journalists to follow Jenny Lind around and report on her comings and goings in the manner of contemporary paparazzi. Barnum himself wrote the first press release, which set the tone of the concert series:

> *"A visit from such a woman who regards her artistic powers as a gift from Heaven and who helps the afflicted and distressed will be a blessing to America."*

He also released a biographical pamphlet which was to be used for publicity, as well as a beautiful photograph with a blurb that emphasized not only her voice but also her good character:

> *"It is her intrinsic worth of heart and delicacy of mind that produces Jenny's vocal potency."*

The furor over her imminent appearance in America was clearly growing, and, in an interview with the *New York Herald*, Barnum claimed:

> *If I knew I should not raise a farthing profit I would yet ratify the engagement, so anxious am I that the United States should be visited by a lady whose vocal powers have never been approached by any other human being, and whose character is charity, simplicity, and goodness personified.*

❦

Even before she left England, Barnum was working hard to create a legend out of this humble Swedish soprano. While waiting for the ship to embark, she gave two charity concerts in Liverpool to large crowds and great acclaim, which was reported in the American papers, and even when on board the paddle steamer *Atlantic*, she gave several concerts for the passengers which was widely reported on and printed in New York. She landed in New York on September 1, 1850, and was greeted by a crowd of "between thirty and forty thousand well-wishers." She endeared herself to the crowd right from the start by kissing the American flag and refusing to let Barnum's coachman clear a way through the crowd with his bullwhip.

Jenny Lind gave two charity concerts on September 11 and 13, 1850, which were not part of the concert tour. For the first concert, she gave her $10,000 artist fee to local charities, and Barnum took advantage of her generosity, going to the stage to tell the audience of her gesture. For the following concert, after she discovered how much Barnum was to earn, she forced Barnum to sell a large number of tickets for two dollars each for the cheapest seats, and one dollar for the standing room area tickets. When Lind found out how much money Barnum, whom she had little personal regard for, was to earn, she forced him to renegotiate her contract and then, after having signed this new contract on September 3, she received her usual $1000 plus and profits over and above Barnum's $5,500.

The tour began in the American eastern seaboard of the United States. She toured in a private railway car to Philadelphia, Boston, Washington, and Richmond, Virginia. Then they set sail for Charleston South Carolina, in which their ship was nearly sunk. After Charleston they sailed to Havana Cuba, and then on to New Orleans for thirteen sold out concerts. From there, they sailed up the Mississippi to Natchez, Memphis Tennessee, St. Louis Missouri and Nashville Tennessee. Thereafter, Barnum presented her in Louisville, Kentucky, Cincinnati Ohio, and Pittsburgh Pennsylvania, where the crowds became unruly, trapping Lind in the concert while they threw rocks at her carriage and into her dressing room. As a result of this distressing turn of events, the tour returned to New York City and then on to

Philadelphia, where the Barnum-produced part of the tour ended, and she went on producing her own concerts.

❧

In the end, Jenny Lind, dubbed "The Swedish Nightingale", performed ninety-three concerts with Barnum, earning $350,000, almost all of which she donated to local charities or to her free schools in Sweden. For his part, Barnum netted at least $500,000.

❧ VII ❧

AFTER JENNY LIND

❄

After the Jenny Lind tour had finished, Barnum was a wealthy man and could well have retired from show business. but retirement was not part of Barnum's makeup and he set about trying to change the public opinion about the American theater. Unlike in Europe, where opera houses were some of the grandest building in any major city, theater in America was associated with a disreputable type of people, thieves, prostitutes, and gamblers. Theaters were frequently cited as dens of iniquity, and consequently there was little to no social capital to be gained by investing in theater in America.

❄

Barnum's methodology was to build the largest, most up-to-date theatre in New York, and called it the "Moral Lecture

Room." At this theatre, he produced the first matinee performances, to encourage families to attend (theater to that point had been exclusively during the evening, and were consequently the site of a great deal of petty crime). These matinees became extremely popular and led to the introduction of the matinee in theater and film presentations.

⚜

The first play he produced was called *The Drunkard*, written by William H. Smith and an unknown co-author, presumed to be Unitarian Minister John Pierpont. Originally produced in 1844, it was the most successful play in the United States until *Uncle Tom's Cabin*, which was also produced by Barnum. Barnum, who had become a teetotaler since his return from Europe, produced this with over one hundred performances. Following this stunning success, he produced a string of melodramas, farces, historical plays and Bowdlerized versions of Shakespeare plays. And then he produced the dramatization of Harriet Beecher Stowe's great novel *Uncle Tom's Cabin*, his most successful show ever. Although much of the power of

the original novel was watered down in the new production, because of certain difficult parts of the play, including the survival of Uncle Tom, the work itself was a huge success, and led to much discussion in the public sphere about slavery and its evils.

❦

The obsessive Barnum began to focus strongly on family-oriented entertainment such as flower shows, dog shows, poultry contests, and other contests, but by far the most popular was the baby contests (the fattest baby, most beautiful baby, handsomest twins, and other types of inexpensive, focus-on-the-family entertainment).

❦

The most popular type of publication in England at the time was known as the "penny dreadful", a pictorial weekly publication that sensationalized crime. Barnum created an American version of this type of publication which he called the *Illustrated News*. He also penned his autobiography which was a runaway best seller, selling more than a million copies. This witty and clever volume, brimming with humorous anecdotes drawn from his colorful life was brilliantly written but, typically of Barnum, short on any kind of verifiable truth.

❧

He also began to invest in property in his hometown of Bridgeport Connecticut, loaning substantial sums to various businesses including the Jerome Clock Company as an incentive to move its factory to his new industrial area there. This turned out to be a terrible idea, and when the company went bankrupt in 1856, most of Barnum's wealth went with it. As often happens in the Americas, when misfortune befalls a man who overreached, Icarus-like, his fall was celebrated by all those who did not have the nerve of guts to try themselves.

❧

Even a man as august as philosopher Ralph Waldo Emerson wrote that Barnum's fall from grace showed "the gods visible again." Despite the many naysayers, there were some people who helped him, including the great General Tom Thumb, now touring and performing on his own. Together, General Tom Thumb and Barnum undertook a European tour. Barnum himself went on a lecture tour as a temperance speaker, to great acclaim and great profit. He was sufficiently successful that by 1860, he had emerged from debt and amassed enough money to build a new mansion, "Lindencroft" (the second of four in Bridgeport) to replace his palace, "Iranistan" which had burned to the ground in 1857, and managed to assume management and ownership of his museum once again as well.

◈

In the following few years, Barnum, built the very first public aquarium in America, built an impressive exhibit called the "Seven Grand Salons" which showed the Seven Wonders of the World, built a rogues gallery of wax figures of criminals, and published a guide book that claimed that there were 850,000 curiosities contained within its walls.

◈

It was at this time that the original Siamese Twins, Chang and Eng Bunker, who had performed for him many years before in the museum, came out of retirement for a short but extraordinarily popular six weeks to perform at the museum, and raised enough money to send their children to college. Barnum also introduced the giantess Anna Swan and the man who was to replace the now wealthy Tom Thumb, a proportional little person known as Commodore Nutt who visited President Lincoln at the White House.

◈

The American Civil War was raging from 1861-65, and Barnum was squarely on the anti-slavery Unionist side of the war. Unlike many of his contemporaries, who feared retribution, Barnum was unafraid to put his money where his mouth was, introducing pro-Unionist lectures, dramas and other exhibits at his Museum. He hired a Unionist female actress named Pauline Cushman who had worked as a spy behind enemy lines to relate her death defying adventures.

She was, predictably, a smash hit. These various and diverse efforts earned him the wrath of an attempted arson by a disgruntled Confederate in 1864, and then on July 13, 1865, the whole museum burned to the ground, likely an arson, although the cause was never actual determined. Unwilling to admit defeat under any circumstances, Barnum re-established the museum at a new location, and this too burned to the ground in March 1868. He did not try to rebuild his museum after this tragedy and finally went out of the museum business.

POLITICS

❧

Even before his museum was burned to the ground, Barnum was considering a run at politics. He had long been a public speaker and writer, and when the American Civil War broke out, issues suddenly seemed more serious and far more important to him as a citizen of the now divided United States. Barnum had previously described himself as a Jacksonian Democrat As with the Jacksonian Democrats, championed by President Andrew Jackson, he was in favor of rights for the common man as opposed to any semblance of aristocracy or favor for the wealthy, the vote for people without land, and an expansion of the territory of the United States (one might call it a pre-Roosevelt Manifest destiny with a social conscience). With the outbreak of the Civil War, the Jacksonian Democrats were not a particularly effective voice for emancipation of the slaves, and so he joined with the fledgling Republican Party, as a progressive.

❃

The association of the Republican Party with radicalism and progressive attitudes may seem strange to a modern reader, seeing as the Republican Party is now associated with conservatism while the Democratic Party tends to be associated with progressive politics. It was not always thus though. At one point the Republicans were comprised of radicals and progressives, bent on tearing down the fabric of the hidebound establishment. Barnum had made a point of coming out on the side of the Unionists, in favor of the abolition of slavery, and of greater rights for men and women, rich or poor, black or white, and consequently joined the new Republican Party, which had been established in 1854 to represent the anti-slavery side. This came about because of his opposition to the Kansas-Nebraska Act of 1854 which created the new territory and would move hundreds of thousands of native peoples and create a state that supported slavery.

❃

In 1865, Barnum ran successfully as a Republican in the Connecticut State assembly. While there, he was a vocal opponent of slavery and a fierce supporter of the Thirteenth Amendment (abolishing slavery). In his stump speeches, he spoke of his own experience with African American slaves with passion, convincing many undecided voters. He ran unsuccessfully for Congress but his stump speeches were filled with regret for the plight of the slaves. In one speech he said that while living in the South:

I whipped my slaves. I ought to have been whipped a
thousand times for this myself. But by then I was
a Democrat—one of those nondescript Democrats,
who are Northern men with Southern principles.

Although there was no particular evidence that Barnum had ever actually owned slaves, his arguments convinced many. In this, as in many other aspects if his life, the truth was slightly less significant than the point he was trying to make. Barnum was finally elected and served four terms in which he was active in many important and progressive (and a few reactionary) ways.

⚜

In 1875, he was elected Mayor of Bridgeport, and was highly esteemed, improving the town immeasurably with gaslight, better water supply and strict liquor laws which included a Sunday closure of all taverns in the town, and better and stronger prostitution laws. But before he became mayor, he had an offer in 1870 from William Cameron Coup to start a travelling circus that would be called "P.T. Barnum's Grand Traveling Museum, Menagerie, and Circus" which was launched in Brooklyn in 1871.

⚜

This circus traveled by train and included animals like elephants (including the famous Jumbo, who sadly was hit by a train many years later in St. Thomas, Ontario, Canada), giraffes, and trained horses and dogs. He also hired a large number of acrobats, clowns, and other human performers. True to his style, he also included "human curiosities" like little people, albinos, and giants, many of whom had worked in his museum in years gone by. From the beginning, Barnum referred to this circus as "The Greatest Show on Earth", an epithet that stuck, and which made Barnum a very wealthy man yet again.

⚜

As was quite common in the nineteenth century, disaster struck his company when, in the winter, Barnum stored his horses and other animals in the Hippotheatron, which was on the site of what would later be Madison Square Gardens. In 1872, this building burned to the ground, killing all his circus animals, and devastating the business. Barnum and his partners, not to be deterred, quickly rebuilt and restocked his circus within only a few months, and went back out on the road.

⚜

The following year, November 19th, 1873, Barnum's long-suffering wife and life partner, Charity, died of heart failure at their home in Bridgeport while he was abroad visiting his friend John Fish in England. At the time, Barnum claimed that he was too grief-stricken to attend the funeral, but then, fourteen weeks later, he married his friend John Fish's twenty-two year old daughter, throwing the veracity of his grief into doubt.

⚜

Possibly because he wanted to spend more time with his new bride, Barnum stepped away from the circus business and decided to run successfully as Mayor of Bridgeport. As a teetotaler, he campaigned against allowing saloons to open on

Sundays, worked hard to install gaslight along the main streets, and threatened the water company with making it a public utility if they did not improve their performance. This threat worked, and he went on to serve as mayor for one very successful term, after which he returned to the Connecticut General Assembly for two more terms. One of the laws that Barnum shepherded through congress was the so-called Comstock Law making "any drug, medicine, article, or instrument" to prevent conception illegal in Connecticut. In today's world, this law came to be viewed as a limit on the rights of the mother, but in the late nineteenth century, it was considered a progressive law that protected women from unwanted pregnancy and death. This law was only struck down in 2018.

❦

In 1876, Barnum formed yet another circus with the group known as the "European Menagerie and Circus" and then in 1880, he brought James A. Bailey on board to form the "P. T. Barnum's Great London Combined." It was for this circus that he acquired a huge elephant known as Jumbo, at eleven feet and thirteen thousand pounds, who became the greatest attraction of this circus. In 1885, Jumbo was struck and killed by a train in St. Thomas Ontario, Canada, and afterward, Barnum displayed Jumbo's carcass for many years. In that year, Barnum and Bailey put their partnership on hold for two years, after which they came together again to create the "Barnum and Bailey Circus", which was his most successful circus and which continued long after his death as America's most popular circus. In 1919, it was purchased by the Ringling Brothers and continued operating until 2017, when pressure from animal rights groups forced its closure.

In late 1890, Barnum suffered a debilitating stroke and was confined to his home. He gave permission to the *New York Sun* to publish his obituary before his death, so he could have a chance to read it. He died on April 7, 1891, at his home in Bridgeport Connecticut, surrounded by friends and family. The death of America's Greatest Showman was met with great accolades, and his reputation continues even to today, despite the fact that he is mostly remembered as a circus ringleader, a role he actually never performed. As with many other great men, "the evil that men do lives after them; the good is oft interred with their bones." So it was with Barnum; many of the deeds that he believed were his best, are remembered today as barbaric or reactionary. Nevertheless, he is undoubtedly a brilliant man and one of the greatest shapers of contemporary American society.

❧ IX ❧

THE BARNUM LEGACY

❧

Barnum pioneered something he referred to as profitable philanthropy, particularly in relation to his hometown of Bridgeport Connecticut. As he put it:

❧

I have no desire to be considered much of a philanthropist...if by improving and beautifying our city Bridgeport, Connecticut, and adding to the pleasure and prosperity of my neighbors, I can do so at a profit, the incentive to 'good works' will be twice as strong as if it were otherwise.

❧

He was instrumental in establishing the first hospital in Bridgeport and served on its board of directors. He was also a major donor to Tufts University in Medford, Connecticut. He was appointed to the Board of Trustees even before the founding of the university in 1852 and made several large donations to the campus; include a fifty thousand dollar donation in 1883 to establish a museum and building for the department of Natural History. It is for this reason that the mascot of Tufts University is Jumbo the Elephant.

⚘

By far his greatest legacy though is in the establishment and shaping of three great American forms of entertainment: the Broadway theater experience, the circus, and the museum. As odd as it sounds, none of these were part of American life in the way that they are taken for granted today. In terms of Broadway entertainment, it was Barnum who established the theater district in Broadway, New York City, and it was he who produced some of the greatest plays of the time in *The Drunkard* and *Uncle Tom's Cabin*. He chose play that were deliberately both entertaining and educational, and, usually, political. Barnum felt strongly that entertainment should both please the audience and teach them something. He paid dearly for his strongly held beliefs too when arsons burned his museum to the ground twice! He also believed strongly that his performers should be treated well and paid well. Although many of his methods would not pass muster in today's society, he sought out performers who had been shunned by the theater and entertainment communities before him - people who would have been referred to as "freaks" were recruited by him and paid handsomely. The fact that they were displayed in politically problematic ways was not a consideration for Barnum. Almost all the performers, whether human oddities like giants, albinos, little people, Siamese twins, four legged women, or bearded women; disabled people like microcephalics, Down Syndrome sufferers, or people born without arms and legs; Native Americans, former black slaves; acrobats, strong men and women; talented singers, actors, jugglers, and musicians - all were paid well and were able to live comfortable lives into retirement. This was unheard of before his time.

❧

In addition, he went to great lengths to legitimize the American theater, which had, up to that time, had closer relationships with criminal elements and prostitution than high society. This is, of course, something it had in common with European theaters that had been associated with itinerant jugglers and beggars, but the new view of the theater as a bastion of wit and intelligence was fostered by the likes of Oscar Wilde in England and others. Barnum's tour of the Swedish Nightingale, Jenny Lind, brought culture to the United States and this tradition took off after him in a way even Barnum himself could never have imagined.

❧

Barnum's museums in New York and Philadelphia made way for the great American institutions like the Smithsonian Institution, the Metropolitan Museum of Art, the Guggenheim, and other great museums and art galleries that thrive in today's society.

❧

His development and curating of the first circuses is a slightly more problematic legacy. He introduced animal shows which have recently come under attack for how they treated these animals. He brought attention to the plight of the American underclass by giving voice to their concerns, and institutions like "Wild Bill's Wild West Show" was strongly influenced by his legacy. He made Americans aware of the plight of the American Buffalo, sadly too late, as the great herds were decimated in the later years of the nineteenth century.

⚜

He had strong views on temperance, and produced plays, gave lectures, and presented events that stressed the importance of temperance to a culture of drunkenness in America in the mid-nineteenth century. The common denominator in almost all of Barnum's work is education. As a largely self-educated man, Barnum was very dedicated to shifting the social discourse from what he saw as destructive discourse like slavery, elitism, and low-class entertainment to elevated topics like the emancipation of the slaves, high culture, social justice, and temperance. While his methods, by today's standards are not particularly palatable, they were groundbreaking in his day. Seeing a personality as large as Phineas Taylor Barnum is difficult to separate from his time. He was one of the most influential men in all of American history; his ideas were used by Walt Disney, the major Broadway theaters, the film industry, circuses of all kinds, carnivals, fun houses, and the sorts of entertainment associated with theme parks and midways.

❧ X ❧
THE QUOTABLE BARNUM

୭❀ଓ

Like many wags in the nineteenth century, Barnum said many witty and wise things. Here are some of the more memorable.

> *"The noblest art is that of making others happy", he said, with full confidence that he was doing just that.*
>
> *He was very interested in the individuality of people - he displayed people because of their individual qualities, saying "No one ever made a difference by being like everyone else."*
>
> *His opinion of the gullibility of the American public was on full view: "Nobody ever lost a dollar by underestimating the taste of the American public" and the better known quip: "There's a sucker born every minute."*

◊※◊

Barnum was full of advice on living the good life. As regards a vocation, he said it but did not practice in his mind.

> "Unless a man enters upon the vocation intended for him by nature, and best suited to his peculiar genius, he cannot succeed."
>
> He went on to describe how to succeed: Whatever you do, do it with all your might. Work at it, if necessary, early and late, in season and out of season, not leaving a stone unturned, and never deferring for a single hour that which can be done just as well now. The old proverb is full of truth and meaning, "Whatever is worth doing at all, is worth doing well." Many a man acquires a fortune by doing his business thoroughly, while his neighbor remains poor for life, because he only half does it. Ambition, energy, industry, perseverance, are indispensable requisites for success in business. Fortune always favors the brave, and never helps a man who does not help himself.

◊※◊

> He also felt that in order to succeed, the simplest and best plan was to do what you love: "The safest plan, and the one most sure of success for the young man starting in life, is to select the vocation which is most congenial to his tastes."

Then, what would lead to the greatest success was not to

compete with everybody, but rather to compete with your competition.

> *He said it this way: "The great ambition should be to excel all others engaged in the same occupation."*

৯৯৯

> *He also was a master of the peculiar, yet true, turn of phrase, including this life lesson: "Be cautious and bold."*

Similarly, he was fond of helping those who helped themselves.

> *To this end, he advised: "The best kind of charity is to help those who are willing to help themselves." In addition, he noted that "Fortune always favors the brave, and never helps a man who does not help himself."*

৯৯৯

> *He felt that much of his own success was due to his extraordinary energy, built on the foundation of good health:*
> *The foundation of success in life is good health: that is the substratum fortune; it is also the basis of happiness. A person cannot accumulate a fortune very well when he is sick.*

৯৯৯

He also felt that debt was ruinous for a businessman. He

himself experienced debt on several occasions, and just like any other man, he found it onerous:

> *Young men starting in life should avoid running into debt. There is scarcely anything that drags a person down like debt. It is a slavish position to get ill, yet we find many a young man, hardly out of his 'teens,' running in debt. He meets a chum and says, 'look at this: I have got trusted for a new suit of clothes.' He seems to look upon the clothes as so much given to him; well, it frequently is so, but, if he succeeds in paying and then gets trusted again, he is adopting a habit which will keep him in poverty through life. Debt robs a man of his self-respect, and makes him almost despise himself.*

❦

> *On the subject of business, which was his passion, he had even more sage advice: "The possession of a perfect knowledge of your business is an absolute necessity in order to insure success."*
> *In business, as with all other areas of his life, Barnum advised control as the single greatest ensurer of success: "Remember the proverb of Solomon: 'He becometh poor that dealeth with a slack hand; but the hand of the diligent maketh rich', and 'I will loose my camel, and trust it to God!' 'No, no, not so,' said the prophet, 'tie thy camel, and trust it to God!'"*

❦

Similarly, the key to much of his own success lay in his ability to *publicize* his work effectively.

> *In true Barnum style, he described it colorfully:*
> *"Advertising is to a genuine article what manure*
> *is to land - it largely increases the product."*

❀

On the other side of the coin, he felt that there was little that could hurt him if properly publicized.

> *On the subject of publicity, he said: "I don't care what*
> *the newspapers say about me as long as they spell*
> *my name right."*

❀

Barnum was fond of the concept of the humbug. A humbug, in his understanding, was not a bad thing necessarily; rather it was a grand gesture that was designed more to enthrall than to be accurate or true.

❀

> *And in what business is there not humbug? 'There's*
> *cheating in all trades but ours,' is the prompt reply*
> *from the boot-maker with his brown paper soles,*
> *the grocer with his floury sugar and chicories*
> *coffee, the butcher with his mysterious sausages*
> *and queer veal, the dry goods man with his*
> *'damaged goods wet at the great fire' and his*
> *"selling at a ruinous loss," the stock-broker with*
> *his brazen assurance that your company is*

bankrupt and your stock not worth a cent (if he
wants to buy it), the horse jockey with his black
arts and spavined brutes, the milkman with his
tin aquaria, the land agent with his nice new
maps and beautiful descriptions of distant
scenery, the newspaper man with his 'immense
circulation', the publisher with his 'Great
American Novel', the city auctioneer with his
'Pictures by the Old Masters' — all and every one
protest each his own innocence, and warn you
against the deceits of the rest. My inexperienced
friend, take it for granted that they all tell the
truth—about each other! and then transact your
business to the best of your ability on your own
judgment.

❧

On humbugs in science, he had just as much skepticism:

Science is another important field of human effort.
Science is the pursuit of pure truth, and the
systematizing of it. In such an employment as
that, one might reasonably hope to find all things
done in honesty and sincerity. Not at all, my
ardent and inquiring friends, there is a scientific
humbug just as large as any other. We have all
heard of the Moon Hoax. Do none of you
remember the Hydrarchos Sillimannii, that
awful Alabama snake? It was only a little while
ago that a grave account appeared in a
newspaper of a whole new business of
compressing ice. Perpetual motion has been the
dream of scientific visionaries, and a pretended

but cheating realization of it has been exhibited by scamp after scamp. I understand that one is at this moment being invented over in Jersey City. I have purchased more than one 'perpetual motion' myself. Many persons will remember Mr. Paine— 'The Great Shot-at' as he was called, from his story that people were constantly trying to kill him—and his water-gas. There have been other water gases too, which were each going to show us how to set the North River on fire, but something or other has always broken down just at the wrong moment. Nobody seems to reflect, when these water gases come up, that if water could really be made to burn, the right conditions would surely have happened at some one of the thousands of city fires, and that the very stuff with which our stout firemen were extinguishing the flames, would have itself caught and exterminated the whole brave wet crowd!

⚜

On independence, which was a hallmark of all his businesses, he said:

Those who really desire to attain an independence, have only to set their minds upon it, and adopt the proper means, as they do in regard to any other object which they wish to accomplish, and the thing is easily done.

⚜

Barnum was sanguine on the subject of money.

He wrote "Money is, in some respects, like fire. It is a
very excellent servant, but a terrible master." But
money alone was not the purpose of business; it
was more a means to enlightenment. He wrote:
"It is the eyes of others and not our own eyes
which ruin us. If all the world were blind except
myself I should not care for fine clothes or
furniture."

❧

On cynicism toward other humbugs, he wrote that
"the greatest humbug of all is the man who
believes—or pretends to believe—that everything
and everybody are humbugs."

❧

Also, on the subject of humbugs in politics:

Politics and government are certainly among the most
important of practical human interests. Now it
was a diplomatist—that is, a practical manager
of one kind of government matters—who
invented that wonderful phrase—a whole world
full of humbug in half-a-dozen words—that
'Language was given to us to conceal our
thoughts.' It was another diplomatist, who said
'An ambassador is a gentleman sent to lie abroad
for the good of his country.' But need I explain to
my own beloved countrymen that there is
humbug in politics? Does anybody go into a
political campaign without it? are no
exaggerations of our candidate's merits to be

allowed? no depreciations of the other candidate?
Shall we no longer prove that the success of the
party opposed to us will overwhelm the land in
ruin? Let me see. Leaving out the two elections of
General Washington, eighteen times that very
fact has been proved by the party that was beaten,
and immediately we have not been ruined,
notwithstanding that the dreadful fatal fellows
on the other side got their hands on the offices and
their fingers into the treasury.'

⚜

On trust in business, he was very honest. He believed that people need to be able to trust each other if they want to do business, and so he was a big fan of the handshake.

You reflect that he is worth twenty thousand dollars,
and you incur no risk by endorsing his note; you
like to accommodate him, and you lend your name
without taking the precaution of getting security.
Shortly after, he shows you the note with your
endorsement canceled, and tells you, probably
truly, "that he made the profit that he expected by
the operation," you reflect that you have done a
good action, and the thought makes you feel
happy. By and by, the same thing occurs again and
you do it again; you have already fixed the
impression in your mind that it is perfectly safe to
indorse his notes without security.

❧ XI ❧

HOW WE CAN USE P. T. BARNUM IN OUR LIVES

❦

In many ways, Barnum's life is a mirror of American society: he was an entrepreneur with ideas that changed the way the world viewed people, science, art, nature, and many other things. He was a man of his time of course. And so many of his methods may seem out of fashion or even offensive to modern ears. Still, he was deeply committed to what he believed were universal human values of fairness, kindness, freedom, and the pursuit of the American dream.

❦

In many ways, Barnum is a man to be admired because he was true to his values, and because he managed to accomplish a great deal that actually changed the character, nature, and trajectory of American life.

❧ XII ❧

THE HUMBUGS OF
THE WORLD

❧❧❧

This book, written in 1866, when Barnum had first become a state congressman, itemizes and exposes many of the most famous hoaxes and humbugs of the nineteenth century world. It is written in the almost Mark Twain like style of the erudite Barnum. He begins the book with the general definition of the word as defined by Webster's Dictionary as a noun: "an imposition under fair pretences;" and as a verb: "to deceive; to impose on." Barnum, a master of the humbug himself, has a slightly broader definition and uses examples of men from all walks of life from the humble churchgoer who pretends he has more money than he does, to the doctor, the actor, the poseur, the dandy, and many others. All of these operate under some kind of false pretense, according to Barnum.

❦

He cites some specific examples, from M. Mangin, the French humbug, who sold black pencils claiming that they would make one into a great artist, if used properly and he had several renderings of his own dandyish likeness plastered all over his coach, parked in the Place de la Bastille or the Place de la Madeleine. Then he drew upon the name of old "Grizzly" Adams, the bear trainer with whom he had had dealings, and even hired to perform in his museum. This man had trained and been mauled by bears for years, and his fortitude was what kept him in business. His entire head was scarred and dented from encounters with these bears, and yet his stock in trade was to make it seem that these bears were not dangerous.

❦

He then relates the story of his beluga whale that he had installed in the basement of his museum, and then had to place lit by gaslight which frightened the whale so much that he hid. Almost every visitor declared either that there was no whale, or that he was made of India rubber or painted. Barnum himself was frustrated by this, by immensely enjoyed the telling.

❦

He describes a number of medical hoaxes that he described as humbugs. These include many of the pills that were being peddled as cures for any number of things, but in fact were sugar pills. Similarly, many of the elixirs that were supposed to cure anything from heartbreak to heart attacks were described in hilarious ways, certain that they were more effective as entertainment than as cures.

He then moves on to the Spiritualists, focusing on the Davenport brothers, a pair of mediums who used every trick available to them. They hailed from Buffalo New York and used music, cabinet secrets, rope tying, and innumerable other tricks to convince people that they could commune with the spirit world. He did not mince words when he categorically debunked these false spiritualists. In the following chapters, he describes various spiritualist phoneys and debunks their many methods, their tricks to fool customers. Barnum describes these with great glee in the entertaining and humorous style Barnum is known for. Found within are discussions relative to hoaxes, money manias, adventurers, medicine and quacks, religious humbugs, trade and business impositions, spiritualists, ghosts and witchcrafts, and personal reminiscences.

THE ART OF MONEY-GETTING;
GOLDEN RULES FOR MAKING
MONEY

ﷺ

Often seen as one of the first self-help books, Barnum could recognize a massive money-maker when saw it. The Art of Money-Getting is a relatively slim volume for Barnum, filled with excellent advice on how to make money in America.

> *It is specifically aimed at Americans in the United States because, as Barnum puts it, "in the United States, where we have more land than people, it is not at all difficult for persons in good health to make money."*

He claimed that the country was uniquely filled with potential fortunes because there were so few people and so much land, and because of this, there were many untapped resources. Europe, the place he consistently compares the United States to, was filled with people who were stuck in occupations that limited them, while the United States had no such barriers to wealth. He begins with the traditional "go for the gold" arguments about choosing a career that you love to working as hard as you can at your chosen profession. More than this, he identified several areas in which there were untapped potentials to be mined. The first was a judicious use of the principles of personal economy – wear your clothes for one more year, shop for food, drink, and tallow candles judiciously. Then, he suggests that you select your vocation carefully; the vocation the others find lucrative may not be the appropriate one for you, he claims. He then identifies debt as one of the largest barriers to making money – it is a hole into which many unwary people fall, and it is one from which it is difficult to climb out of because of the necessity of being indebted to someone who has a stronger desire to be wealthy than you do. He stresses the importance of perseverance, because it is the one thing even the penniless man can have that will distinguish him from others who are "born tired."

۞

Further to this, he advises not to borrow money from relatives, not to rest on your laurels, and not to think less of others who work hard, and then he goes on to lay out the absolute importance of advertising. It is important to know the world around you, and so, he says, you much read the papers. Knowing what is changing is paramount in discovering the key to profit. They often lie just behind the headlines. He gives the example of "Genin, the hatter" who was the first person to purchase a ticket to see Jenny Lind when these tickets were offered for auction. Nobody had ever heard of Genin the hatter before this auction, but when he outbid many of the denizens of Fifth Avenue. After it was known that this humble hatter had outbid all the wealthy

New Yorkers, his name was suddenly well-known and a Genin hat became a must-have item for these wealthy people.

۞

He goes on to give advice like be polite to your customers, to be charitable (in which he advises helping those who help themselves), and the importance of "blabbing". One must never tell one's business secrets, he claims. Many businessmen seem willing to tell others about the sad state of their business dealings; this is seriously dangerous. Finally, he says, you must preserve your integrity. If you follow these easy steps, you will be wealthy. This is a slim volume, and it is intended for a business audience. Brevity was not a quality often associated with Barnum, but this volume was his slimmest, and, other than his autobiography, his best selling.

❧ XIII ☙

BOOKS BY BARNUM

❦

Barnum, Phineas Taylor, *The Life of P. T. Barnum*, New York: the Courier Company, 1855; London: Sampson Low, Son, & Co., 1855

❦

The Humbugs of the World. An Account of Humbugs, Delusions, Impositions, Quackeries, Deceits and Deceivers Generally in all Ages, London J.C. Hotten 1866

❦

Struggles and Triumphs or, Forty Years' Recollections, edited and abridged by Carl Bode, New York: Penguin, originally published by Warren, Johnson & company, 1872

The Art of Money-Getting; Golden Rules for Making Money, New York, Armada Press, 1880

Lion Jack, a Story of Perilous Adventures Among Wild Men and the Capturing of Wild Beasts, New York: G.W. Dillingham Co., 1887

Animal Stories: An Account of the Author's Famous Expedition in Search of Wild Animals for the Circus, New York: Saalfield, first edition, 1926

❧ XIV ❦

BOOKS ABOUT BARNUM

෯෯

Betsy Golden Kellem, "Showman: The True Story of P. T. Barnum and Jenny Lind", in *Vanity Fair*, December 22, 2017

෯෯

Harris, Neil. *Humbug: The Art of P.T. Barnum*, University of Chicago Press, 1981

෯෯

Kunhardt, Philip B. Jr., Kunhardt, Philip B. III, and Kunhardt, Peter W., *P. T. Barnum: America's Greatest Showman*, New York, Alfred A. Knopf, 1995

YOUR FREE EBOOK!

As a way of saying thank you for reading our book, we're offering you a free copy of the below eBook.

Happy Reading!

GO WWW.THEHISTORYHOUR.COM/CLEO/

Made in the
USA
Columbia, SC